An Advanced Discussion-Based ESL Curriculum

Of Bananas & Hard-Boiled Eggs

Thriving in a Foreign Culture through
the Journey toward Biculturalism

Mary Lou Codman-Wilson, Ph.D.

WESTBOW
P R E S S
A DIVISION OF THOMAS NELSON

WestBow Press books may be ordered through booksellers or by contacting:

WestBow Press
A Division of Thomas Nelson
1663 Liberty Drive
Bloomington, IN 47403
www.westbowpress.com
1-(866) 928-1240

Because of the dynamic nature of the Internet, any web addresses or links contained in this book may have changed since publication and may no longer be valid. The views expressed in this work are solely those of the author and do not necessarily reflect the views of the publisher, and the publisher hereby disclaims any responsibility for them.

Any people depicted in stock imagery provided by Thinkstock are models, and such images are being used for illustrative purposes only.

Certain stock imagery © Thinkstock.
Cover and interior art work by Katie Alford.

ISBN: 978-1-4497-3575-3 (sc)
ISBN: 978-1-4497-3574-6 (e)

Library of Congress Control Number: 2011963335

Printed in the United States of America

WestBow Press rev. date: 2/28/2012

To my ESL students who worked on each stage of this curriculum with me.

Anyone who knows only one culture knows no culture. In coming to know a second or third culture, one discovers how much that was taken to be reality is actually an interpretation of realities that are seen in part and known in part; one begins to understand that things assumed to be universal are local; one realizes that culture defines both what is valued and which values will be central and which less influential."

David Augsburger, *Pastoral Counseling across Cultures*, 1986, p.18.

Contents

Preface

In centuries past, people stayed within their own national borders and often had little contact with "outsiders." But most people in the twenty-first century can and do interact with those from very different cultural and language backgrounds. Many of the major cities of the world have become multicultural. This intermingling can lead to the journey of changing identity. People can be released from the mono-cultural ethnocentrism that comes from being surrounded continually by those of the same ethnic and cultural heritage and language group. The intermingling of cultures is actually one of the unique advantages of living in a globalized world. We can choose to have our horizons expanded, our values strengthened, and our life experiences broadened as we interact with people very different from ourselves.

When one moves intentionally to a "foreign" country, intermingling is part of daily life. But it is never automatic. People have to choose to move beyond their cultural heritage; they have to choose to live with understanding of those who are different. They have to choose to "enter another's worldview, sharing that consciousness, exploring its interior, looking out at the wider world through its windows while retaining one's own worldview." [1] People have to choose to become fluent in two languages and cultures. When they do, they are able to share their unique gifts and make a significant contribution in the land they now call home. But it is always a choice.

My husband and I and our two small children lived in Austria for a year. His school district in Maryland sent him to become a curriculum consultant at the American International School in Vienna. We arrived with no knowledge of German and spent the year learning about the culture. But we lived on the outside of the lives of the residents of Vienna because we could not converse well in German. Therefore, we stayed in our English-speaking "cocoon," with our relationships limited to other English-speaking foreigners. We never felt a part of Austrian life or made a significant contribution to Austrian people or culture.

In contrast, I have worked for years with immigrants who have come to the United States to make this their new home. They are here permanently. Many have engaged with life in the dominant culture and have settled comfortably into the routines of bicultural living. Yet others have lived separately because of their limited English conversational ability and reticence to move out of their ethnic cocoon. This has affected their quality of life and inclusion in the broader society and allowed for few genuine friendships with Americans who are not from their culture of origin. This ESL conversation curriculum for English speakers is a way to give these immigrants support

---

[1]   Augsburger, *Pastoral Counseling across Cultures, 39.*

and empower them to move beyond their culturally safe cocoon and grow as people who can engage with those in the dominant culture.

Foreign language-speaking adults who thrive in the dominant culture can also better understand and connect with their children who quickly assimilate into the values of their friends in the mainstream culture. Many immigrants fear their children will forsake their culture of origin, so they endeavor to keep their children contained in their ethnic cocoon. This strategy can lead to alienation between first and second or second and third-generation immigrants in a new culture. It serves a family's health and well-being much better to choose the values and priorities they consider best in the dominant culture and incorporate them alongside the values and priorities they want to maintain from their family heritage. The adults who are journeying toward biculturalism can also help their children who are engaged in that same bicultural identity process.

This open, welcoming approach to cross-cultural living is called acculturation, not assimilation. "Acculturation focuses on the interplay of two or more cultures, or world views, with possible changes in each. By contrast, assimilation is the absorption of a minority culture into the dominant culture and a subsequent denuding of the minority's identity and heritage. It is one-way change."[2] In assimilation, people lose their distinctiveness as they seek to blend into the dominant culture. In acculturation, people can learn how to live in terms of the values and priorities of another culture without losing their distinctiveness. This is the journey of bicultural identity. When minority peoples learn how to speak and act comfortably in the dominant culture, this will enable them and their families to acculturate appropriately without assimilating and losing their roots and unique heritage. Proper acculturation is critical for immigrants because the lack of acculturative adjustment, identity formation, and their well-being as minority people create insecurities and crises of life for them. People's fear of those insecurities or life changes is what can keep them in their ethnic "cocoon," frozen in the traditional values and lifestyle of their culture of origin. The alternative is to explore engagement in the dominant culture of their new country. Such engagement requires a proficiency in the dominant language of the host culture.

Still, the amount of acculturation people experience is a choice. I have chosen to change as I internalized many of the exceptional values of the Asian peoples and cultures with whom I have been engaged. One Chinese international student was in a seminar I co-taught with an Asian Indian in the United States. Midway through the seminar, the student gave this assessment of me to the whole class: "I know who you are," he said to me. "You are a hard-boiled egg. I am Chinese. I am yellow on the outside (Chinese looking), but I am white on the inside (with Caucasian values). You are white on the outside but yellow on the inside." That's the origin of the title of this book: *Of Bananas and Hard-Boiled Eggs, an ESL Curriculum on the Journey toward Biculturalism*. The Chinese student's statement was a great compliment to me because he could see how Asian values were evident in my behavior, in what I emphasized in the teaching of that seminar, and in how my Asian colleague and I co-taught and interacted together.

---

[2]   M.L. Codman-Wilson, <u>Thai Cultural and Religious Identity and Understanding of Well-Being in the US</u> (Unpublished dissertation, Northwestern University, 1992).

There are several terms used in cross-cultural literature to describe the change in identity many people experience when they are engaged in cross-cultural living. Some people use the term "bicultural." This means I am part my culture of origin and part the new culture I have internalized. For the sake of simplicity, that is the term being used in this curriculum. It describes people who move in and out of the dominant culture in their new setting and are able to mix values and behavior from both their culture of origin and their new culture. Bernard Adeney, in his thought-provoking book *Strange Virtues: Ethics in a Multicultural World,* says: **"As we live in another culture, our goal is to become bicultural--to become fluent in two languages and two cultures"**[3]

Other people describe those involved in this identity journey as "third-culture people." This is technically a more accurate representation of the process of identity formation. Third-culture people live close to the boundary of two cultures and can cross over from one to the other culture with relative ease. But as they cross back and forth, they create a new composite identity within themselves. Such people are no longer solely people of their culture of origin; it is evident they are different from the values and behavior of their heritage. But they also are not recognized as legitimate people of the culture they have internalized since they are not of that culture by blood or heritage. They are a synthesis—a third-culture people—with a composite identity that mixes differently for each person. The term third-culture kids (TCK) is used in the literature to talk about children who are born with a certain racial identity but who have been raised in another culture. Often that second culture of their formative years is the one they identify with more closely. Yet each person creates his or her own unique cultural synthesis.

Whether you speak of this cultural journey of identity as the journey toward biculturalism or the journey toward third-culture identity, the journey itself is one of the benefits of our globalized world. People who want to be relevant in such a world and who want to thrive in a foreign culture will be able to do so when they are able to go in and out of the mainstream culture comfortably. They will be able to make friendships and contributions in the dominant culture while still maintaining their roots and friendships in their culture of origin.

This curriculum has been developed for that goal—to help people grow in confidence and in English language usage so they can cross over easily and often. It has been developed to help people adapt to life in the dominant culture and not be limited to life within their ethnic cocoons.

It is a long, hard process to become bicultural; all who are courageous enough to take the journey need a support system. Having an English language discussion-based group can provide that needed support and encouragement so the students will persevere together and not give up. The rewards in their lives, in the lives of their families, and for the people they engage in the dominant culture will be well worth the effort.

Many thanks to all who have walked beside me in my cross-cultural relationships and partnerships; to those who have been my teachers relationally and academically; to my husband, Keith, who

---

[3] Bernard T. Adeney, Strange Virtues: Ethics in a Multicultural World (Downers Grove, IL: Intervarsity Press, 1995), 72

has journeyed with me through the years; to Katie, my administrative assistant, who has helped prepare the materials and artwork for publication; and to Marti and Carol and my editing team at Westbow Press.

Mary Lou Codman-Wilson, Ph.D.
Chicago, Illinois 2011

Introduction

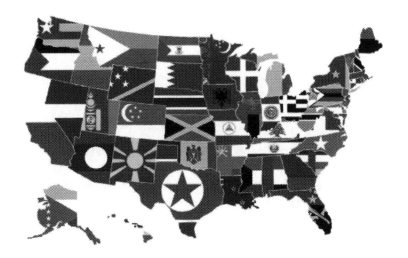

America is a *pluralistic society*. It is common to hear many different languages when one goes shopping or banking or even walks around in one's neighborhood. ESL classes help people of these different language groups learn how to communicate in English.

There are many ESL curriculum choices for those at beginner and *intermediate* levels. This curriculum is more advanced, designed for those who are able to discuss in conversational English the problems they face daily in a foreign culture.

The goal of this advanced English conversation curriculum is to help ESL learners *mainstream* into the *dominant* culture and develop a *comfortable bicultural identity* so they can be at home in both their culture of origin and their new "foreign" culture. The *expectation* is that through English conversation practice and discussion of topics that are *relevant* to them, learners will develop the *confidence* to move outside the *cocoon* of their own language group and *interact successfully* in English in the daily *routines* of life because they understand English and can be understood by English-speaking people. (Please note: vocabulary words are in italics)

The topics in this book are grouped under two major headings. Chapters 2 through 6 are focused on communication issues. Chapter 2 is on the importance of asking questions. Chapter 3 is about the need to build trust in cross-cultural relationships. Chapter 4 describes the *various* ways people communicate "no" in their cultural context. Chapter 5 deals with understanding children's report cards in the American public school system. And chapter 6 *handles* how to talk to medical personnel.

Chapters 7 through 17 deal with issues faced in cross-cultural living and the process of *bicultural identity* formation. In chapter 7, the discussion centers on stereotypes. Chapter 8 deals with the problem of *discouragement* in language learning. Chapter 9 draws some lessons from geese about the importance of teamwork in language learning. Chapter 10 provides a *self-evaluation* progress check so students can see how they are growing in their language learning and cross-cultural adaptation. Chapter 11 *involves* the students in role-plays of incidents in daily living. Chapter 12 gives helpful advice about finding a job. Chapter 13 discusses the common problem of depression for people who are struggling to adapt to a foreign culture. Chapter 14 discusses cultural differences in the understanding of time and calendars. Chapter 15 is about understanding American values. Chapter 16 is about maintaining one's own cultural traditions. And chapter 17 is on developing a *bicultural identity*.

The vocabulary and comprehension sections in each lesson were developed from real-life stories central to each topic. A team that included ESL learners wrote these stories about *issues* they experienced while learning how to live *successfully* in a foreign culture. Vocabulary definitions were chosen with ESL level-three learners in mind for ease of understanding. The curriculum is discussion based and gives learners the opportunity to discuss their feelings and support one another in their cultural adjustment.

Other features of this curriculum:

- The *format* of each chapter is built around one of the themes in the curriculum.
- That theme is presented in a story.
- Vocabulary words that may be new to the students are italicized in the story. By highlighting the vocabulary words in the story, the learners can go back to the story and see those words in *context*.
- In chapters 1 through 7, definitions are given by each word.
- By chapter 8, when the students are more advanced in English *comprehension,* there is a mix and match exercise where students match the correct definition to the vocabulary word.
- There are also comprehension questions after each story.
- There are sentences the learners need to write using the vocabulary words in that chapter.
- There are discussion questions that encourage the learners to share about how they have faced the topic of the chapter in a practical way in their lives.

Vocabulary

(to) Adapt—to change to fit into your surroundings
Bicultural—combining two cultures
Cocoon—a sheltered environment that is protected and safe
Comfortable—freedom from care; feeling good
Comprehension—understanding
Confidence—feeling sure of one's abilities or in the abilities of another
Context—the setting of words that helps you know what a word means
Discouragement—feeling like you can't do something
Dominant—having power and control
Expectation—something you assume will happen
Format—the way a chapter is put together
(to) Handle—to take care of
Identity—who you are; the characteristics and qualities that define a person
(to) Interact—to work with someone or something
Intermediate—between beginner and advanced; in the middle
Issues—topics people discuss or problems people face
(to) Mainstream—to become part of the dominant culture
Opportunity—a chance to learn or to do something you didn't know or that is new
Pluralistic society—a society where there are many different races, languages, religions, and cultures
Relevant—something that is related and that applies to the person
Routines—things you do every day; normal, repeated patterns
Self-evaluation—to review one's own effectiveness
Stereotypes—a common picture in your head about a group of other people
Successfully—doing something well
Various—different kinds of ways

Comprehension

1. What is the goal of this curriculum?

2. Why is it important that this curriculum is discussion based?

Discussion

1. What are some values you have appreciated in your new culture?

2. Why is it important to move out of one's national language cocoon?

3. What does it look like to be out of the cocoon and mainstreaming into the dominant culture?

4. Discuss what a comfortable bicultural identity would be for you.

5. What would a comfortable bicultural identity be for your children?

Chapter 1

Adjustment to Life in a New Country

The main goal when adjusting to life in a new country is to go from being a *visitor* to feeling like the new country is home; you belong there. The first key is a desire to relate meaningfully across cultures. This was illustrated by our granddaughter meeting the daughter of a Taiwanese international family we knew. Wen Huang was at Northwestern University when I was; we were both working on our Ph.D. degrees. Both little girls were at the age to investigate and reach out to each other. That's the key to *adaptation* in another culture. There must be a willingness to go beyond the familiar and learn to engage with those of other cultures. It is a mental choice. The desire to connect acts as a bridge to create understanding between people of *different* cultural backgrounds.

The following stories by people adjusting to life in the United States from their life in another country *illustrate* some of the issues involved.

Question: *Describe a value from your home culture that you miss.*
Answers:

1. "When I came to the United States, I came with my husband because we were married in Mexico before we came to the United States. We went to California and lived there for more than a year. After that, we moved to Indiana. When we came to the United States, sometimes I felt sad because I didn't have my family with me. I only had my husband's family. My brothers lived in Washington. As for now, I think I have gotten used to being only with my daughters and my husband since I have been living in Indiana for eleven years."

—Yolanda, mid-forties, from Mexico.

2. "I came to the United States about eight years ago from Mexico . . . I miss my family, my friends, and the *lifestyle* I had in Mexico. I haven't seen my family and friends for a while. I miss my mom's cooking, being all together, and spending time with them. I miss going out with my friends. I also miss the warm and long days in Mexico."

—Augustine, late twenties, from Mexico

A teenager's perspective:

"Every culture is *different*. Whether you like it or not, it is the way it is. The most *important* way for me to *adjust* to the new culture and feel more comfortable with it is the *motivation* to really work on it. It requires hard work. You really have to push yourself. Let your emotions lead you into getting better at adjusting to the new culture; don't get *discouraged*.

"My goal before I moved to the United States to study was to be *adjusted* to the culture and language in three months. As time went by, I *realized* after the first semester that I felt like I really lived here, not that I was a *visitor* for a period of time . . . I've learned you need to *engage* in every social event *available* in your community. There are events and sports programs that you can attend at local park districts. There are also garage sales where you can meet your neighbors and maybe talk about something you have in common with them after looking at what they have to sell.

"I think cross-cultural *adjustment* needs *bravery*, hard work, and most important, faith. God can do anything in your life. Take everything as a lesson. You cannot do it by yourself."

—Widiante Moestopo, a teenager from Indonesia

Vocabulary

Adaptation—to change to fit into your surroundings
(to) Adjust—to change in order to fit
Available—can be gotten, had, or used
Bravery—courage
Different—not the same; unique
Discouraged—feeling like a failure; being ready to give up
(to) Engage—to be involved in
(to) Illustrate—to picture the truth in a situation
Important—something that means a lot or has value
Lifestyle—the way one lives
Motivation—desire or drive toward a goal
(to)Realize—to understand
Visitor—someone who comes and then leaves, does not stay

Choose five of these vocabulary words and write a separate sentence for each word.

1. _____

2. _____

3. _____

4. _____

5. _____

Comprehension

According to the stories, what makes *adjustment* to life in the United States hard?

What are some keys to success from the teenager's story?

Discussion

What changes have you made in order to live in your new country?

What do you need to do to go from feeling like a visitor in your new country to making your new country your home?

Chapter 2

Ask . . . Ask . . . Ask!

To learn how to live *successfully* in another culture, you need to learn how people *communicate*, what they *value,* and what their actions mean. To do that, you need to ask many questions. You will learn the most about your new culture from the people who are the *majority* in that culture instead of just asking your own culture group what they think things mean. It may take *courage* to ask questions, but those in your new culture will want to help you learn and understand them, so they are usually happy to help answer your questions.

If you do not ask what things mean, you may make a wrong *assumption*, as Dayna did.

Story

"Not too long after I moved into my new apartment in Taiwan, I came home to find lots of reddish spots on my patio. The spots looked like dried blood. Since there was a security person standing close by my unit, I walked over to him and asked, 'What *happened?'* I thought someone may have been hurt on my patio. The guard's English wasn't very good, and I couldn't express myself well in Chinese either; I just kept *pointing* to the spots and asking, 'What is this?' He just told me he would take care of it.

"A little while later, I went outside and there were workmen mopping up my entire patio. One of my neighbors who spoke English was in the courtyard, and I went back out and asked her what was going on. She laughed at me and told me that the spots were not blood but betel nut juice. Workers had been working on the roof and were spitting from above. Because I had 'complained,' the guard made them come and clean up their mess. She told me that the guard would never have made the workers clean up like that except for the fact that I was a foreigner. After this, I learned to be careful in how I phrased my questions and whom I asked so I would not make *unnecessary* trouble for other people. I would have cleaned up the mess myself if I had only known what it was!"

—Dayna Wheatley lived in Taiwan for a few years when her Chinese husband was working there. They later came back to the United States, where she met him originally.

Rini and her husband came to the United States from Indonesia so he could study for his Ph.D. at the University of Wisconsin. They are now back in their home country of Indonesia, and she teaches Indonesian to foreigners in her country. This is her advice:

"Living abroad brings you face to face with a *different* culture and *customs*. It is better if you get some information first about the country you will be staying in before you leave your home country. But whatever information you get, don't depend on it 100 percent, and don't *generalize* it. Never think that every *citizen* in that country will do the same things you have been told.

"For example, I was told before I came to the United States that Americans are always *direct*. But when I was in the States, it was not always the case. I once worked at a *convalescent center*. One time one of my coworkers told me that some of the nurses were *'talking about me behind my back.'* At that time I was a little bit *shocked* because I thought if there was something wrong with me, they would tell me directly instead of talking about me behind my back. From that *incident,* I *concluded* that I can't *generalize* everything.

"Accept the differences in culture and customs with an *open mind and heart.* Do your best to learn many new things so you can communicate what you really mean. Learn to understand and copy the expressions, the body language, the pronunciation, etc., those in the dominant culture use. Just keep asking the *citizens* of that country about the *customs* or the expressions you do not understand. You will be *fascinated* by all the different answers you get."

—Rini Moestopo, Indonesia

Vocabulary

Assumption—something we think or do without checking the facts
Citizen—belonging to a country, usually by birth
(to) Communicate—to speak or make one's meaning known
(to) Conclude—to use what we know to make a decision
Convalescent center—a place where people get help after an illness or injury

Courage—bravery
Customs—things people do as part of their culture
Different—not the same; unique
Direct—honest, straightforward
Fascinated—very interested; surprised
(to) Generalize—to take one incident and say it is true for everyone or everything
(to) Happen—to take place
Incident—something that happens
Majority—more than half of the total
Open mind and heart—a willingness to accept new ideas
(to) Point—to show where something is (call attention to)
Shocked—very surprised, often unpleasantly surprised
Successfully—doing something well
"Talking about me behind my back"—gossip
Unnecessary—not needed
(to) Value—to see something as important; to treasure

Comprehension

Choose seven of these vocabulary words and write a separate sentence for each word.

1. _____

2. _____

3. _____

4. _____

5. _____

6. _____

7 _____

Discussion

1. What did people tell you about the United States before you came?

2. How are those ideas the same as what you found? How are they different?

3. What do you want to understand about the majority group's actions or attitudes in your new country?

4. Why does it take courage to ask questions?

Chapter 3

Building Trust

Artist: Peggy Sanders for <u>Bridges</u> Cross-Cultural Quarterly, vol. 1 # 9, Building Trust

This lesson involves questions and answers throughout, so you will notice a change in the usual *format* of the chapter.

To have good relationships with people outside your culture, you need to *build trust* in each relationship. Trust is the ability to *rely* on another person. It is feeling *safe*, comfortable, *welcomed*, and understood with another. For example, if I hire a babysitter *I am trusting* the babysitter to take as good care of my children as I would.

When do you feel safe with another person?

Can you think of an example of trust?

To build trust, I need to understand what another person is saying and what that person means. Otherwise, I can *misinterpret* his or her meaning.

How do you know if you've understood what the other person has said?

The American Indians have a wise saying: "If you want to understand another person, you need to *walk a mile in his or her moccasins.*" In other words, you need to try to *experience* life as others do.

> What would you need to do to try to experience life the way someone who is from another culture does?

I can build trust by saying, "I need your help so I don't *lose face*" and then seeing how I am helped.

> What keeps you from asking an English speaker to help you?

I can also build trust by spending time with another person and working on *similar goals.*

> What is one goal you have this year for your life? How can you work together with an English speaker to *achieve* that goal?

> How do you build trust with an English speaker?

> What does an English speaker need to do for you to trust him or her?

Vocabulary

(to) Achieve—to earn a reward; success
(to) Build trust—to work to understand another person so I am comfortable with him or her
(to) Experience—to be exposed to, involved in, or affected by something
Format—the way a chapter is put together
(to) Lose face—feel ashamed
(to) Misinterpret—to have a wrong meaning for what is said
(to) Rely—to have confidence in someone
Safe—secure, free from harm
Similar goals—working to achieve the same things
(to) Walk a mile in their moccasins—to be able to understand what people are feeling
Welcomed—invited into a person's life or home

Choose five words and write a separate sentence for each word.

1. _____

2. _____

3. _____

4. _____

5. _____

Chapter 4

Saying No

Story

"In our Japanese culture, we don't say no or yes *directly*; it is *impolite*. So it is very *awkward* for us when we come to an American home and the *host* says, 'What would you like—coffee, tea, or water?' It takes a lot of energy to respond positively, so we will say, 'Everything is welcome for us, so please choose for me.' When we care so much for another's feelings and want to continue a good relationship, we will try to follow the other's lead in our responses and make him or her happy. But American hosts often want to give you what you really want, so they will ask the same question again. Then we don't know what to do . . .

"In a similar way, if an American says once, 'Please come to my house,' that is usually a *genuine* invitation and he or she expects an answer to that direct invitation. But we often *hesitate*. In Japanese culture, it is polite to say, 'Please come to my house,' but the real invitation is not there. It is just a polite way to show *respect*. Therefore, a Japanese person will say, 'Please come' three or four times; then you know he or she really wants you to come and you will be there."

—Dr. Michiko Takahashi (visiting scholar in the United States from Japan)

The Japanese are not the only ones whose culture is *indirect* in saying yes and no. There are many ways people will try to communicate no without being direct. It may be by words, gestures, or actions. Here are some common ways of communicating no.

1. To *hesitate*, lack *enthusiasm,* or be silent
2. To present an *alternative* offer
3. To *postpone* a decision
4. To blame a third party or an outside circumstance for *rejection* of a *proposal*
5. To *avoid* a direct response
6. General acceptance but without any action on specifics
7. To shift the discussion to another idea or proposal

—adapted from *Managing Intercultural Negotiations*,
Pierre Casse and Surinder Deol (pp.145-46)

Vocabulary

Alternative—a choice between two or more things
(to) Avoid—to keep away from; to keep from happening
Awkward—feeling uncomfortable, embarrassed, or ashamed
Direct—honest, straightforward
Enthusiasm—happiness or interest about something
Genuine—real and true; not fake
Harmony—living and working well together
(to) Hesitate—to pause or stop momentarily; to be unsure
Honesty—Saying what one really thinks or feels, what is true
Host—the person who invites you to his or her home or party
Impolite—rude, not respectful
Indirect—to avoid a straightforward answer
(to) Postpone—putting off until later; to delay
Proposal—a suggested plan
(to) Reject—to refuse to accept, agree to, or believe
Respect—to show honor and special favor

Choose seven of these vocabulary words and write a separate sentence for each word.

1. _____

2. _____

3. _____

4. _____

5. _____

6. _____

7. _____

Comprehension

1. Many Japanese people do not say yes or no directly because it is considered _____.

2. What do the Japanese look for before they respond?

3. What do you feel like when Americans speak directly to you or to others?

Discussion

1. Discuss some ways you say no indirectly.

2. In a specific instance when you said no indirectly, did the person you were communicating with get the meaning you hoped for? Why or why not?

3. How can you balance *harmony* and *honesty* in your relationships?

Chapter 5

Children's Report Cards

Most immigrants who come to the United States want their children to succeed in school, and many immigrant children succeed admirably. Parental help and *encouragement* are needed for that success, however, so it is important to understand the skills and the attitudes on which a child will be graded in public school.

In the United States, students are graded on their *performance,* on how well they *comprehend* various *subject matter* (reading, math, social studies, language arts, health, spelling, writing, etc.), and on their attitudes and relationships with other students that come under the headings of work habits, *citizenship*, and responsibility. Work habits describe the way a student listens in class, follows instructions, works independently and quietly when told to, and does assignments neatly and on time. Citizenship describes acting with *respect* toward others. Responsibility describes the tasks or duties one is expected to do.

Here is a *sample* report card (from fourth grade in a Wheaton, Illinois, public school)[4]. This is only page one; page two has *effort* and achievement for science/health, social studies, physical education, music, and art. An understanding of each word used in the grading system is necessary in order to help your child meet the standards for homework assignments, encourage important attitudes and work habits, and be able as a parent to speak in English with the child's teacher at parent–teacher conferences.

The vocabulary in this lesson is longer than in other chapters so that all the words on a grade school report card can be understood. **Suggestion: Allow two to three sessions for this lesson.**

---

[4]   Copyright www.cusd200.org.

STUDENT

⭐ Work Habits, Citizenship, and Responsibility

	1st Quarter			2nd Quarter			3rd Quarter			4th Quarter		
	Consistently	Frequently	Needs Improvement	Consistently	Frequently	Needs Improvement	Consistently	Frequently	Needs Improvement	Consistently	Frequently	Needs Improvement
Follows directions												
Uses time constructively												
Completes assigned work on time												
Writes legibly in daily work												
Is prepared for class												
Demonstrates organizational skills												
Works independently												
Demonstrates self-control												
Is respectful toward others												

Listening and Speaking

Listens attentively												
Responds appropriately												
Participates actively												
Expresses ideas clearly												

🕐 Reading

EFFORT	1	2	3	4
ACHIEVEMENT				

Word Analysis — ACHIEVEMENT
- Applies word analysis and vocabulary skills to comprehend selections
- Demonstrates fluent oral reading

Literal Comprehension — ACHIEVEMENT
- Fiction Text – summarizes and identifies story elements and sequences
- Nonfiction Text – identifies main idea and supporting details

Inferential Comprehension — ACHIEVEMENT
- Forms opinions, makes predictions and connections, draws conclusions

✏️ Writing

EFFORT	1	2	3	4
ACHIEVEMENT				

Written Communication — ACHIEVEMENT
- Composes a variety of writing pieces
- Writes in a well-organized and coherent manner
- Supports writing with details
- Uses writing process strategies (prewriting, drafting, revising, editing, final copy)

Writing Skills — ACHIEVEMENT
- Uses conventions (punctuation, capitals, paragraphing, spelling)
- Demonstrates an understanding of correct grammar skills

ⓐⓑ Spelling

EFFORT	1	2	3	4
ACHIEVEMENT				

- Masters lessons/tests — ACHIEVEMENT
- Applies spelling knowledge in written work — ACHIEVEMENT

➗ Mathematics

EFFORT	1	2	3	4
ACHIEVEMENT				

Computation/Accuracy
- Addition/Subtraction — ACHIEVEMENT
- Multiplication — ACHIEVEMENT
- Division — ACHIEVEMENT

Concepts
- Problem solving — ACHIEVEMENT
- Measurement — ACHIEVEMENT
- Number sense (estimation, place value) — ACHIEVEMENT
- Fractions — ACHIEVEMENT
- Geometry — ACHIEVEMENT
- Data collection, graphing, probability — ACHIEVEMENT
- Early algebraic understanding (e.g., patterns, variables) — ACHIEVEMENT
- Communicates understanding verbally or in writing — ACHIEVEMENT

Vocabulary

Appropriately—in the right way for your setting
Assigned—something given to do
Attentively—carefully, with one's full attention
Citizenship—acting with respect toward others
Clearly—easily understood
Coherent—makes sense
(to) Complete—to finish
Comprehension—understanding
Constructively—in a positive and helpful way
(to) Demonstrate—to show
Effort—how hard you try to do something
Encouragement—Words or actions that give a person courage and confidence
(to) Express—to speak or share one's thoughts or feelings
Fluent—to speak and think clearly in another language
Independently—doing something or acting or thinking by oneself, not including others
Inferential—understanding the meaning that is being indirectly expressed
Legibly—in a way that is easy to read
Literal—true to fact
(to) Master—to learn a skill or subject very well
Organizational—putting into working order; arranging according to a system
(to) Participate—to join others in doing something
Performance—how one carries out responsibilities or tasks
(to) Respect—to show honor and special favor
Sample—a part of something representing the whole
Self-control—control over one's actions or feelings
Sequences—what comes one after another
Strategies—skillful plans
Strengths—areas of power; things one is good at
Subject matter—areas of learning in school like mathematics, social studies, and reading
Tardy—to be late
Work habits—how a person does work in a class environment or independently

Comprehension

Choose ten of these vocabulary words and write a separate sentence for each word.

1. _____

   _____

2. _____

   _____

3. _____

_____

4. _____

_____

5. _____

_____

6. _____

_____

7. _____

_____

8. _____

_____

9. _____

_____

10. _____

_____

Discussion

1. What does it mean to help your child "use his or her time constructively" in terms of his or her homework assignment?

2. What does it mean in school for a child to demonstrate self-control?

3. How can you help your child to answer questions out loud and "participate actively" in the classroom?

4. How are those expectations of active participation different from the schooling you experienced in your home country?

Discuss how you can help each other prepare for parent–teacher conferences and be comfortable in dialoging with your children's teachers about their work.

Chapter 6

Talking to Medical Personnel
(Doctors and Hospitals)

Story

"When my five-year old son was playing at the playground, he fell and hit his head hard on the ground. He began to cry. He said his head *hurt* and his arm hurt badly too. There was a big *bruise* on his head, and he was holding his hurt arm with his other hand. I decided to take him to the *emergency room*. The doctor *examined* his head and his arm and *ordered X-rays* for his arm to be sure he had not broken his wrist. I couldn't understand everything the doctor and nurses were saying to me, so I am glad there was a *translator* there who could tell me what they said in my language. After that I knew I needed to attend English classes more *regularly!*"

—Luisa, Mexico

Vocabulary

Bruise—a hurt on some part of the body
Emergency room—the part of the hospital you go to when you need immediate health care
Examined—looked at closely
(to) Hurt—to feel injury or pain

Ordered—commanded
Regularly—something done again and again at a scheduled time
Translator—someone who explains the words in another language
X-rays—pictures of the inside of the body

Discussion

Hospital Situations: Describe a time you needed to go to the hospital.

1. Why did you go?

2. What happened when you were there?

3. What problems did you face?

4. What would help you prepare better for hospital visits in the future?

5   In class, write down what you would say if you have to take your child to the doctor. You can choose what the medical problem is. Each member of the class should read out loud how he or she has explained the problem to the doctor and what questions he or she will ask the doctor.

A Helpful Suggestion: Take the time to write out all of the questions you may have for the doctor to be sure you understand everything before you go see a doctor or go to the hospital.

Name the parts of the body.
What sickness is related to each body part?

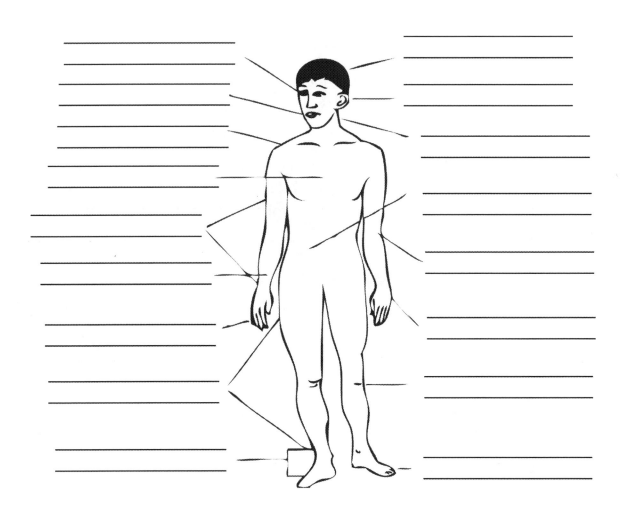

Chapter 7

Stereotypes

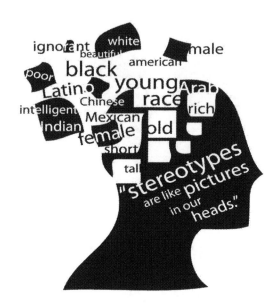

Story

"I first became involved in the Asian Indian community in Chicago at the invitation of a local Indian *leader*. In my first year in the community, two *tragic* incidents occurred. Two different Indian college students, who had been raised in the United States and were studying in universities in the States, each committed *suicide* on their college campus. In both cases, they had fallen in love with a student on their campus their parents rejected as an acceptable marriage partner. The Indian students were *victims* of *generational tensions* in their immigrant families.

"In an effort to become a *bridge person* between traditional Indian parents and the children they were raising in the United States, I became *committed* to the Indian community. Over the years, I wore *saris whenever* I was with the Indians. An Asian colleague and I held 'Growing Up in America' seminars to discuss the tensions between *generations*. I was involved every week in a local Indian Christian church. I went to India at the invitation of several Indian leaders to learn more about their culture from them. A mission organization invited me to do *research*. I went with a *team* of Asian Indians from Chicago to look into the needs of the Asian Indians in the suburbs of London, England. I earned a master of theology in Hindu, Buddhist, and Christian dialogue and a Ph.D. on Asian immigrant *identity* issues in America.

"But in the end, my hopes of working as a bridge person between the Asian Indian generations were not able to be fully realized for two reasons.

"First, I was not an Asian Indian by blood, so I was not considered part of the extended family, and conflicts are usually *resolved* by other family members. That is an important cultural norm I had not understood. Second, Indians *assumed* because I was *Caucasian*, I did not understand their issues and could not be of help. I was *stereotyped* because of my race."

—Mary Lou Codman-Wilson, Ph.D.

Vocabulary

Match the vocabulary words on the left with the correct meaning on the right.

1. _____ Assume

2. _____ Bridge Person

3. _____ Caucasian

4. _____ Committed

5. _____ Generation

6. _____ Generational Tensions

7. _____ Identity

8. _____ Leader

9. _____ Research

10. _____ Resolved

11. _____ Saris

12. _____ Stereotype

13. _____ Suicide

14. _____ Team

15. _____ Tragic

16. _____ Victim

17. _____ Whenever

Definitions

a. To kill yourself

b. Traditional Indian women's clothing

c. A group of people who work together

d. Someone who tries to connect different people or groups

e. A white person of Western European origin

f. Something that brings suffering

g. Promise to do something; dedicated to a long-term course of action

h. A common picture in your head about a group of other people

i. Someone who directs or guides other people

j. To take for granted; suppose something to be a fact

k. Careful study and investigation in some field of knowledge

l. Anytime

m. Someone or something killed, hurt, or suffering because of something that happens

n. Average period of about thirty years between the birth of one family level and the birth of the next

o. Conflicts between people of different generations

p. Decided; gave an answer to a problem

q. Who you are; the characteristics and qualities that define a person

Comprehension

1. Why did the Indian college students commit suicide?

2. Why was Dr. Mary Lou stereotyped?

3. What was the result of her being stereotyped?

Discussion

1. How do you think the parents of those students who committed suicide might have reacted to their children's deaths?

2. Have you ever felt stereotyped? Describe the situation. How did you feel?

5. How can we change people's stereotypes?

Chapter 8

Persistence and Discouragement

Nearly all language learners face the wall of *discouragement* as they learn and then try to *master* a new language. Perhaps you feel *defeated* by your mistakes and the times people did not understand you or you could not remember the right word to say in a conversation. You remember when you felt *embarrassed*. Or you remember times when you were *frustrated* when English speakers spoke too fast or with an accent you didn't understand or used words you didn't know. If you think mostly about these hard times in your language learning, you can get *discouraged*. At those times, it seems better just to take the easy road and speak mostly in your native language. It is easier to avoid trying to make *genuine* friendships in your new culture, fit into the mainstream life of the new culture, and use your English every day. It is easier to say, "I'm too old," "I'm not smart enough," "I won't use my English enough," or "It's not worth all this effort." *Discouragement* takes over your mind, and you feel like a *failure,* so you give up.

But learning English is like learning any new sport or skill. Everyone who is trying to become a musician or an artist, or who is trying out for a sports team, knows he or she must *practice* every day. Athletes must train their muscles and their minds to develop the skills they need. My grandsons play American football. During the football season, they go to a two-hour practice three times a week after school. They also play games in competition on one or two days during the weekends. Last summer our oldest grandson had football camp. In the hot Chicago weather, five days a week, he went to practice and learned team plays, how to *tackle*, run, and throw the ball—all the time wearing his heavy uniform and padding that would protect him as teammates *tackled* each other in *practice*. It was hard work in that heat and humidity, but he kept at it because he wanted to play on the best team. The teams were all ranked according to the skills, ages, and weights of the players, so he worked hard to *master* the skills he needed.

In the same way, there are many levels of language learners. You can learn a language just enough to *survive* in a new culture. When my family and I lived in Austria for a year, I had two small children at home and could not attend German classes, so I only learned enough German to go to the stores and buy what we needed or say the casual, "Good morning," "Good evening," or "How are you?" No one from Austria invited us into their homes to talk with them because we couldn't speak enough German to carry on a conversation. Also, my husband worked in an American International School, so he spoke English all day long. Our social contacts were from that school and all in English, and we attended an international English-speaking church. We remained in our English-speaking *cocoon*. We knew we were only visitors in that country and would be returning to America within the year, so survival German was all we thought we needed. We had not come to make Austria our home for many years.

But when you do come to make your home in the United States, you will *thrive* if you become a *fluent* English speaker. That requires *persistence* so you will have new friendships, new jobs, new opportunities to participate in the culture, and new ways you can make a contribution in your new country. Persistence means you keep learning and using the new language. It will be well *worth the effort*. Eventually you will become *fluent* in English.

Vocabulary

Match the vocabulary words on the left with the correct meaning on the right.

1. _____ Cocoon

2. _____ (to be) Defeated

3. _____ Discouraged

4. _____ Discouragement

5. _____ Embarrassed

6. _____ Failure

7. _____ Fluent

8. _____ (to be) Frustrated

9. _____ Genuine

10. _____ (to) Master

11. _____ Mistakes

12. _____ Persistence

13. _____ Practice

14. _____ (to) Survive

15. _____ (to) Tackle (in American football)

16. _____ (to) Thrive

17. _____ "Worth the effort"

Definitions

a. Feeling like you can't do something

b. To learn a skill or subject very well

c. Repeating exercises to develop skill

d. To grow in a healthy way

e. To stop another person or throw him to the ground

f. A sheltered environment that is protected and safe

g. Able to speak and think clearly in another language

h. To be ashamed, uneasy

i. To live at the most basic level

j. Unsuccessful in obtaining a desired outcome

k. Real and true, not fake

l. To keep at something without giving up

m. Something that is incorrect or wrong

n. To lose

o. To feel blocked or unable to achieve what you want

p. The work you put into something is rewarded

q. Feeling like a failure, ready to give up

Choose seven of these vocabulary words and write a separate sentence for each word.

1. _____

2. _____

3. _____

4. _____

5. _____

6. _____

7. _____

Comprehension

1. Why is it easy to become *discouraged* as you learn a new language?

2. What is needed to *master* that language?

3. What role does *practice* play in language learning?

4. Why is *persistence* needed?

Discussion

1. Can you share a story of when you used a wrong word or phrase in English and were frustrated? What happened?

2. What is most helpful to you as you work hard to *master* your new language?

3. List five ways you can practice your English comprehension and language usage each day.

Chapter 9

Lessons from Geese

There are five important lessons that immigrants can learn from the behavior of geese:

FACT 1
Geese fly in a V *formation*. As each goose *flaps* its wings, it helps to lift up the wings of the birds that follow.

LESSON: People who share a common direction and sense of community can get where they are going. An ESL class can become a group that helps each student become a good English language speaker. We students are all moving in the same direction.

FACT 2
When a goose falls out of *formation*, it loses the lifting power of the bird in front of it. It discovers the problems of flying *alone* and moves back into *formation*.

LESSON: If we want to learn English, we will stay in class with those headed where we want to go and accept the help of other people.

FACT 3
The bird at the front of the *formation* experiences the most wind *resistance*. When it *tires*, it moves to the back of the *formation* and another goose takes the lead.

LESSON: When we have found a job, it is good to help our coworkers succeed with their jobs.
FACT 4

Geese flying in formation *honk* to *encourage* those ahead of them to keep up their speed.

LESSON: We need to *encourage* people to get better jobs or our children to get better grades at school. We also need to *encourage* the other students in the class with us to keep using their English every day.

FACT 5

If a goose gets sick or *wounded*, two other geese drop out of *formation* and go down to the ground with it. They stay with that goose to *protect* it until it recovers or dies. Then they join another group of geese flying overhead or catch up with their original *flock*.

LESSON: We need to stand by each other in *difficult* times until a crisis is past.

—Lessons from Nitzia, Mexico

Information on the behavior of geese adapted from:

Hainsworth, F. Reed. "Precision and Dynamics of Positioning by Canada Geese Flying in Formation." *Journal of Experimental Biology* 128 (1986): 445-62. Web. 13 Jun 2011. <http://jeb.biologists.org/content/128/1/445.full.pdf+html>.

United States. *Everyday Mysteries: Why Do Geese Fly in a V?*, 2010. Web. 13 Jun 2011. <http://www.loc.gov/rr/scitech/mysteries/geese.html>.

Vocabulary

Match the vocabulary words on the left with the correct meaning on the right.

1. _____ Alone

2. _____ Difficult

3. _____ Encouragement

4. _____ (to) Flap

5. _____ Flock

6. _____ Formation

7. _____ (to) Honk

8. _____ (to) Protect

9. _____ (to) Resist

10. _____ (to) Tire

11. _____ Wounded

Definitions

a. Hurt

b. Group of birds

c. Pattern

d. To be weary, to lose energy

e. To lift wings up and down

f. Hard

g. To make a loud noise

h. To shield from danger

i. Words or actions that give a person courage and confidence

j. To fight against somebody or something

k. By itself or oneself

Choose seven of these vocabulary words and write a separate sentence for each word.

1. _____

2. _____

3. _____

4. _____

5. _____

6. _____

7. _____

Discussion

1. What is most interesting to you about the behavior of geese?

2. What lesson from the behavior of geese is most helpful in your mastering of English?

3. How can you apply these lessons from geese to your own life as a language learner and in your relationship with other language learners?

Chapter 10

Self-Evaluation Progress Check

Achieving your goals

1. For each part of this question, rate yourself in one of these three ways:
    N=Needs improvement   S=*Satisfactory*   E=Excellent

    First, in understanding spoken English:
    N   S   E

    Second, in being able to communicate your basic ideas in English:
    N   S   E

    Third, in being able to have a conversation with an English-speaking person:
    N   S   E

    Fourth, in being able to establish a friendship with an English-speaking person:
    N   S   E

2. What level of English language learning do you want to achieve? (Be specific)

3. By what time—name month, year, etc.?

4. What areas do you need to work on?
    Vocabulary?
    Pronunciation?
    Comprehension?

5. How will you work toward achieving your goals? (Give four specific steps.)

6. How will you *assess* your progress?

7. What study habits will you use to achieve your goals?

8. How can this class help you realize your goals?

Vocabulary

(to) Assess—to measure; to evaluate
Satisfactory—acceptable

Chapter 11

Role Plays of Incidents in Daily Living

Role-plays are mini-dramas.

Role-playing is an important way to use your English and talk about *situations* you face daily. In *role-playing,* each person takes a part and acts out what you would say (in English only) if you were in that situation. You make up your *script.* Some *suggestions* are given in each scene. Get into groups of two or three and take fifteen minutes to *practice* what you want to say in your particular role-playing situation. You will do that role-play in front of the class, and each person should speak loudly, slowly, and clearly. Please use *complete* sentences and the best English you can, but communicate a positive relationship with the other person as well. Decide how you will do that. We will build vocabulary words from each scene. Enjoy!

Scene 1: Parent/teacher conference at school

Teacher's concerns (to be spoken about as you decide. You can include other issues as well):
> Child is not talking in class
> Child is drawing at her desk and not listening
> Homework is late
> Parental help with her homework

Parent's concerns:
> She talks a lot at home.

How can I make homework *interesting?*
How can I know if she has homework?
How can I help?
How is she relating to the other children?
What grades is she getting?

Scene 2: A job interview

Employer's questions to be included in the interview:
Skills?
Experience?
Why should we hire you?
Talk about hours, work *expectations, environment*

Potential employee's responses:
Demonstrate willingness to do the job—*prove* why you should be hired
Answer questions in full sentences—speak clearly
Ask questions of your own about the job and the company

Scene 3: Parent/child disagreement

Child's concerns: I want to do something (you decide what) that some of the other children are doing. *Defend* that position.

Parent's concerns: explain why you don't want him or her to do this
Provide *creative alternatives* (i.e., "You can't do this, but you can do that.").
Work at building trust and letting the child know you understand.

Scene 4:

You create a different role-playing situation that you face in daily living and act that situation out with your partner.

Vocabulary

Match the vocabulary words on the left with the correct meaning on the right.

1. _____ Alternative

2. _____ (to) Complete

3. _____ Creative

4. _____ (to) Defend

5. _____ Environment

6. _____ Expectation

7. _____ Interesting

8. _____ (to) Practice

9. _____ (to) Prove

10. _____ Role-playing

11. _____ Script

12. _____ Situations

13. _____ Suggestions

Definitions

a. Second choice

b. Our surroundings

c. The combination of circumstances at a given time; incidents that happen

d. Something you assume will happen

e. Ideas that are given for a situation

f. To make or do something new, showing imagination and inventiveness

g. To show or demonstrate that you are capable or that something is a fact

h. The written words to speak; the copy of a text

i. Acting out a role

j. To stand for, speak on behalf of

k. Repeating exercises to develop skill

l. Gets your attention or curiosity

m. To finish

Additional vocabulary words from role plays:

1.

2.

3.

4.

Discussion

1. Which of these role-played situations has been the hardest for you? Why?

2. What advice can you give to your classmates to help them manage their difficult situations?

3. Discuss some of the issues of parent/child disagreements you have faced in your home. What did your children want to do? Why did you let them do that or refuse to give your permission?

4. How can you and your children work out a good solution?

Depending on the size of your class, this chapter may take more than one session. Be sure there is adequate time to talk about the issues people face in each role-playing situation. Perhaps they will think of additional situations they would like to act out as role plays.

Chapter 12

Finding a Job

Story

"Finding a job is a very *important* way to become *self-sufficient* in a new country. In many families, when both the husband and wife have a job, the family will be fine. Without jobs, the family doesn't have money for rent, for bills, and most important, for food—especially for the children.

"When we don't find a job, we can become angry and depressed. We need help from other people to find a job, especially when we arrive in the United States and don't speak English. It is impossible to get a job if other people don't help us. Then when we have a job, we can help other people find a job.

"For example, when I was looking for a job, I asked many people what companies were hiring. One man told me about a company that had openings. I applied, and after five days someone called me at home to offer me a job.

"The day after I began work, a lady at the bus stop was crying and asking everybody where she could to go to find a job. I told her about the company that just *hired* me and gave her the office address. She went to the office and applied for the job, and the next day she and her husband were *hired*. Now all their family is happy."

—Irene, Mexico

To apply for a job as a nonstudent, you need to create your *résumé*. It has six parts:

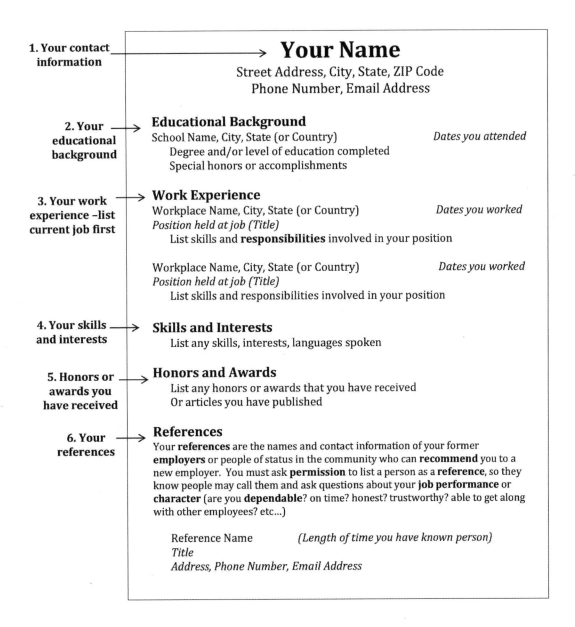

1. Your contact information

Your Name
Street Address, City, State, ZIP Code
Phone Number, Email Address

2. Your educational background

Educational Background
School Name, City, State (or Country)   *Dates you attended*
    Degree and/or level of education completed
    Special honors or accomplishments

3. Your work experience – list current job first

Work Experience
Workplace Name, City, State (or Country)   *Dates you worked*
Position held at job (Title)
    List skills and **responsibilities** involved in your position

Workplace Name, City, State (or Country)   *Dates you worked*
Position held at job (Title)
    List skills and responsibilities involved in your position

4. Your skills and interests

Skills and Interests
    List any skills, interests, languages spoken

5. Honors or awards you have received

Honors and Awards
    List any honors or awards that you have received
    Or articles you have published

6. Your references

References
Your **references** are the names and contact information of your former **employers** or people of status in the community who can **recommend** you to a new employer. You must ask **permission** to list a person as a **reference**, so they know people may call them and ask questions about your **job performance** or **character** (are you **dependable**? on time? honest? trustworthy? able to get along with other employees? etc...)

Reference Name   *(Length of time you have known person)*
Title
Address, Phone Number, Email Address

Creating a Résumé:

In order to work in the United States, you will need a social security number or a visa that *allows* you to work. Student visas *usually restrict* students to work only on their college campus. Companies who hire immigrants will usually offer a *work permit* if the person doesn't already have one.

_____

_____

_____

Educational Background

Work Experience

Skills and Interests

Honors and Awards

References

Vocabulary

Match the vocabulary words on the left with the correct meaning on the right.

1. _____ (to) Allow

2. _____ Character

3. _____ Dependable

4. _____ Employer

5. _____ (to be) Hired

6. _____ Important

7. _____ Job performance

8. _____ Permission

9. _____ (to) Recommend

10. _____ Reference on a résumé

11. _____ Responsibilities

12. _____ (to) Restrict

13. _____ Résumé

14. _____ Self-sufficient

15. _____ Usually

16. _____ Work permit

Definitions

a. How well you do on a job

b. Means a lot; has value

c. A person who hires a worker for salary

d. To be independent; to trust oneself

e. To give consent

f. Moral qualities inside you

g. To apply some limits

h. A person who offers information about you or a recommendation about you

i. Reliable all the time

j. Most of the time; often

k. Job profile (picture of who you are); summary of your education, skills, and work experience

l. To be employed for a job; to get paid for a job

m. Paper giving permission for work

n. Tasks and duties one is expected or has agreed to do

o. To say okay; to give permission

p. To speak positively of someone or something

Comprehension

Choose seven of these vocabulary words and write a separate sentence for each word.

1. _____
   _____

2. _____
   _____

3. _____
   _____

4. _____
   _____

5. _____
   _____

6. _____
   _____

7. _____
   _____

Discussion

1. Why is a résumé helpful?

2. Why are references important?

3. Describe to the class how you found a job.

Homework:
Create your résumé, and bring it to class next session.

Chapter 13

Depression

Artist: Emerson Frey, A Disciple's Bifocals: 1988. Unit 2, pg. 32

What is *depression*? Try to define it in your group.

Story

"*Occasionally,* we have all felt downhearted or sad, but this is especially common when we have just arrived in a new country. Then we remember all the important things we left behind: our family, our things, our cultural *lifestyle.* We are also faced with so many things that are unfamiliar—in language, *customs,* and patterns of daily life. We may feel out of place, like a fish out of water. Over time these feelings of strangeness and *isolation* can lead to *depression.*

"Depression is a serious sickness. It makes you feel hopeless, *inferior,* and *inadequate.* Many people who are depressed need *treatment* to get out of negative feelings. Some people with depressive illness never look for *treatment.* They think they are just sad because they miss their family or they don't speak English. But depression is more than sadness. It takes away your energy and your hope and takes over your body and your mind. You don't enjoy things that you always used to enjoy. Depression hurts you and everyone around you.

"For many people depression *disappears* when they find a job and when they meet people from other countries and realize they have passed through the same problems. It helps to *think positively* and try to find a class to learn English and try to do new things. If these things definitely do not work, we need to go to a doctor to get *anti-depressive medication*. We need to get help for the sake of our family, so we will be better tomorrow.

"As we adjust to our new culture, we need *patience, encouragement,* and *emotional support*. We also need to offer our time to help other people *overcome* their depression."

—Irene, Mexico

Vocabulary

Match the vocabulary words on the left with the correct meaning on the right.

1. _____ Anti-depressive medication

2. _____ Customs

3. _____ Depression

4. _____ Disappears

5. _____ Emotional support

6. _____ Encouragement

7. _____ Inadequate

8. _____ Inferior

9. _____ Isolation

10. _____ Lifestyle

11. _____ Occasionally

12. _____ Overcome

13. _____ Patience

14. _____ (to) Think positively

15. _____ Treatment

Definitions

a. Medication for depression

b. To think about good things, not bad things

c. Feelings of sadness, hopelessness, inadequacy

d. Not good enough enough in comparison to others

e. Not able to complete a task successfully

f. Words or actions that give a person courage and confidence

g. Goes away

h. Help provided to get better from sickness

i. Sometimes, not always

j. Providing help to people in their troubles

k. Working through problems without complaining

l. To defeat a problem

m. The way you live

n. Things people do as part of their culture

o. Separation from

Choose seven of these vocabulary words and write a separate sentence for each word.

1. _____

2. _____

3. _____

4. _____

5. _____

6. _____

7. _____

Comprehension

Put true or false on the line beside each sentence.

1. Depression is a common problem for people in a foreign culture. _____

2. Depression is not a serious sadness. _____

3. It is possible to get well from the depression. _____

4. Depression medication can help with the symptoms. _____

5. Depression makes you feel happy. _____

6. Depression causes problems in your family and in your job. _____

7. It is not good to admit you are depressed. _____

Discussion

1. Why do people not say they are depressed?

2.   What have you done to get help when you were depressed?

3.   What have you missed most in coming to this new country?

4.   What is worse in your new culture?

5.   How do you confront your disappointments?

Chapter 14

Time and Calendars

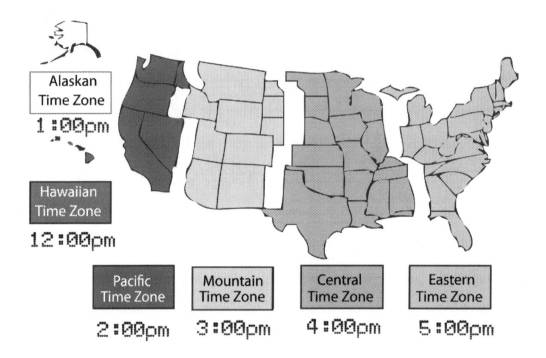

At 2:00 a.m., Sunday, November 7, 2010, the clocks were set back one hour. This is our fall time change. We say the clocks fall back (an hour) in the fall and spring forward (an hour) in the spring. Here is a story by an *international* student who did not know about that time change.

Story

"I came to Wheaton College from Nigeria in September 1999. Nigeria is on the west coast of Africa. It is located four to fourteen degrees north of the equator and three to fourteen degrees east of the equator. Almost throughout the year, the day and night are equal. The sun rises at about 7:00 a.m. and sets at about 7:00 p.m. The country has only two *seasons,* in contrast to summer, winter, fall, and spring in the United States. The two seasons are the rainy season and the dry season. The weather is *constant* and *predictable*.

"I had to *struggle* to *adjust* to the American weather in Wheaton, Illinois. I found it *difficult* to sleep when I looked out through the window and saw the sun rising in the sky and the time was only 4:00 a.m. In the summer, the sun can be shining very bright. I would think it was 4:00 p.m., only to discover it was already 8:00 p.m.

"I had the greatest *shock* one day in 1999 when I went to class at 11:30 a.m. by my watch and found the classroom empty. I was *surprised*. The students were not in the class, and the professor was not there. I thought I was too early, so I waited for fifteen minutes and nobody came. Then I went to the office of the professor and said, 'Excuse me, sir! Why is nobody in the class?' The professor laughed and then told me that I had to adjust my watch because the time had been set back by one hour."

—Ven. Dr. Felix Erondu, Nigeria

Vocabulary

Match the vocabulary words on the left with the correct meaning on the right.

1. _____ (to) Adjust

2. _____ Constant

3. _____ Difficult

4. _____ International

5. _____ Midnight

6. _____ Predictable

7. _____ Seasons

8. _____ Shock

9. _____ (to) Struggle

10. _____ (to be) Surprised

Definitions

a. Not changing; remaining the same

b. A sudden, bad surprise

c. Hard

d. To experience something unusual or unexpected

e. A student or businessperson from one country visiting another country

f. The patterns of the weather in a year

g. Twelve o'clock at night, the middle of the night

h. To make one's way with great effort, to work hard

i. To change in order to fit

j. Something you can count on because it is the same each time

Choose seven of these vocabulary words and write a separate sentence for each word.

1. _____
2. _____
3. _____
4. _____
5. _____
6. _____
7. _____

Comprehension

1. Why was nobody in the class?

2. Did the professor get mad at this Nigerian student?

3. How do you know the correct time?

4. Do you have different seasons in your home country?

5. How long is it daylight in your country each day?

6. How have you had to adjust to the weather or the time in your new country?

Discussion

Write a paragraph in class describing an incident when you had to adjust to time in your new country. Each student will read his or her paragraph out loud in the class.

Chapter 15

Understanding American Values

Story

"After being in the United States for over fifty years, I still find it difficult to remember names and to use people's names in a normal, friendly conversation. In the country I came from, you use a name when you scold someone, when you call someone to get their attention, or when you address a certain person in a group situation. Otherwise, you don't. But here in the United States, it is considered polite to say people's names more often. They say it makes people feel you are interested in them. For example, my American husband would say, 'It's so nice to see you again, Susan.' I figure Susan already knows her name, so why remind her? But it makes her feel special, and that is considered important in America."

—Grete Shelling, Austria

1) Other American values are in the picture above. How is each of the values below represented in the pictures?

   a. *Materialism*—the drive toward a comfortable life, usually supported with credit card purchases

b. The *pursuit* of pleasure—seen in many TV advertisements *promoting* various products or *destinations* for vacation (like Disneyland or Las Vegas)

c. The importance of each individual's rights and freedoms—this is the *foundation* of *democracy*

d. *Achievement* and success based

e. *Romantic* love

f. *Punctuality*—being on time

g. *Fast food*—big business

h. *Individualism*—living life making one's own choices and doing what one wants

To live successfully in another culture, we need to understand the *dominant values* of that culture. Values are the *unseen prompter* behind behavior that might seem strange or different. Understanding other people's values is important because people in our new culture will expect our *behavior* to *conform* to their values.

Vocabulary

Match the vocabulary words on the left with the correct meaning on the right.

1. _____ Achievement

2. _____ Behavior

3. _____ (to) Conform

4. _____ Democracy

5. _____ Destinations

6. _____ Dominant

7. _____ Foundation

8. _____ Materialism

9. _____ Polite

10. _____ Promoting

11. _____ Punctuality

12. _____ Pursuit

13. _____ (to) Remind

14. _____ Romantic

15. _____ (to) Scold

16. _____ Unseen prompter

17. _____ Values

Definitions

a. Success; to earn a reward

b. Supporting a product, an idea, or a person

c. Something you build on

d. Someone or something (not seen) who directs your behavior or gives you cues about what to do or say

e. Having power and control

f. To reprimand or discipline someone

g. To cause someone to remember or think of something

h. How a person acts

i. The social principles held or accepted by an individual, class, or society

j. An emphasis on possessions and a comfortable life

k. To go after something, someone, or some goal

l. To fit into

m. Respectful and having good manners

n. Love that is based on an emotional attraction

o. A society based on the equal rights of all people

p. Being on time

q. Places you go to

Comprehension

1. Why is it good to say a person's name in normal conversation in the United States?

2. In class, write several sentences on the value of democracy. Read your sentences out loud to each other and discuss them.

Discussion

1. What values in the United States do you think people expect you to conform to? Give examples.

2. What are the problems you experience with the values of materialism and the pursuit of pleasure?

3. Describe how some of the other values have affected you or your children.

4. How are these values different from the values of your home culture?

Chapter 16

Maintaining Your Cultural Traditions

Story 1

When you go to live in a foreign country, there are many of your *cultural traditions* that you will want to *maintain*. Grete Shelling of Austria writes:

> "When my parents, sisters, and I moved from Austria to the United States, we brought with us candle holders that you could clip onto the branches of a live Christmas tree. It took some time to find the right size candles that fit, but we did! Having lit candles on the tree is an important tradition to *maintain* because it reminds us of our childhood when we had no electric Christmas tree lights. In Austria, after we sang several Christmas songs, we blew out the candles on the lower *branches* first, then the ones on the higher branches. I was the youngest, and so my daddy would pick me up so I could *blow out* the highest candles. Then the regular lights were turned on, and we got to see our Christmas presents under the tree. To this day, my sisters and I still light candles on our live trees every Christmas Eve. My American husband is a little *nervous* about that, so he always places a pail of water and a *fire extinguisher nearby*, just in case one of the candles *tips over* and begins to burn down our house. But in all these years, that has never happened. Until it does, lighting candles on a Christmas tree is one *custom* from the 'old country' that I *refuse* to give up."
>
> —Grete Shelling, Austria

However, there are some cultural traditions that you cannot maintain in your new country. The following story is from the book *The Journey of the Lost Boys* (of Sudan) and *describes* the *shock* those boys had when they were told they could not have many wives in America.

Story 2

"'I will go to Africa and I will bring back ten wives,' declared one Lost Boy with emotion.

'Not if you plan on living in America,' I answered. 'And should you one day perhaps return to Africa and bring ten wives back to the United States with you, I suggest you get to know them really well on the return flight. Because when you land in America, you're going to have to pick your *favorite* one and kiss the others goodbye.'

'I am a grown man now!' he *shouted*. 'Who will stop me? What can they do?'

'I know you don't want to hear this,' I *continued*, 'but an American judge can stop you. It is the law of our land, and if you refuse to *comply* with his orders, he can even throw you in jail.'

My friend turned angrily to walk away."[5]

---

[5]   Joan Hecht, <u>The Journey of the Lost Boys</u>, (Allswell Press; 2005), 128.

Vocabulary

Match the vocabulary words on the left with the correct meaning on the right.

1. _____ (to) Blow out (candles)

2. _____ Branches

3. _____ (to) Comply

4. _____ (to) Continue

5. _____ Cultural traditions

6. _____ Customs

7. _____ (to) Describe

8. _____ Favorite

9. _____ Fire extinguisher

10. _____ (to) Maintain

11. _____ Nearby

12. _____ Nervous

13. _____ (to) Refuse

14. _____ Shock

15. _____ (to) Shout

16. _____ (to) Tip over

Definitions

a. To fall down

b. Worried

c. To keep on going

d. Close

e. To tell about

f. A sudden, bad surprise

g. Ways people act in your home country

h. Things people do as part of their culture

i. The arms of a tree

j. To say no

k. To talk very loudly

l. To put the fire out

m. To accept or go along with

n. Special to you; something you like very much

o. Keep (on doing)

p. A canister you use to put out fires

Choose six of these vocabulary words and write a separate sentence for each word.

1. _____

2. _____

3. _____

4. _____

5. _____

6. _____

Comprehension

1. Why did Grete choose to have lit candles on her Christmas tree in America?

2. What does her American husband think about her tradition?

3. Why can the Sudanese man from Africa *not* have many wives in America?

4. What did he think about that?

Discussion

1. *Describe* two *cultural traditions* you have maintained in your new country.

2. Why are they important to you?

Chapter 17

Bicultural Identity

One of the greatest *benefits* of living in a culture that is very different from your *culture of origin* is the opportunity to develop a *bicultural identity*. A person with a bicultural identity can go back and forth *comfortably* between two different cultural worlds. This enables a person to *mainstream* into the dominant culture. It keeps people from being *isolated* in their culture of origin's language group. Children of parents who live cross-culturally often make this adjustment quickly and can develop a bicultural identity as they go to school, but that can cause generational issues because children adapt to new cultures faster than adults.

This is the situation of many immigrants, especially if they came to a foreign country as children. Often the original family members who have immigrated to a new country maintain their language, live separately from people in the "new" country, and raise their children with the same expectations and values that were *relevant* in their home country. They stay within the *cocoon* of their original culture and do not mix easily or often with those of the new country. But when their children attend a public school in this new country, these children are surrounded by the values of their *peers*—values that are often different from the values at home. The immigrant children then begin to act according to the values of their peers.

This has created *tension* between the generations—a tension of identity and belonging. But that tension can be eased if people learn to become bicultural. Every culture has strengths and weaknesses. Bicultural people will *recognize* the strengths of the new culture and choose to *adapt* those to their own lives, alongside the strengths of their culture of origin. This allows them to *appreciate* both cultures and become *bridge people* between those in their culture of origin and those in the dominant new culture.

For example, through my work among Asians for decades, I have *internalized* many of the values that I *admire* from different Asian cultures. I intentionally move toward Asians in any mixed cultural group to get to know them and talk with them. I have studied Asian religions, societies, and value systems. I am grateful that I have been changed by Asian values, culture, and spirituality. Yet I am not fully Asian. My culture of origin is still Anglo-Saxon. I am seen on the outside as a white American, but in truth, I am a person in-between. My *choices* and *identity* reflect both Asian and Anglo-Saxon values. I am like a hard-boiled egg.

All of us who are merging two or more cultures in our identity have learned how to be *comfortable* relating to people from our own family background and to those of other cultural backgrounds. This process of *adaptation* takes work. But its *rewards* are greater than the struggles. A bicultural person can *thrive* best in a multicultural setting and bring the most *harmony* and hope to our *fractured* world. Bicultural people have the *privilege* of building bridges between cultures. They can break down hurtful *stereotypes* and help *diverse* people work together for *mutual understanding* and *social justice* in the world.

Vocabulary

Match the vocabulary words on the left with the correct meaning on the right.

1. _____ (to) Adapt

2. _____ (to) Admire

3. _____ (to) Appreciate

4. _____ Benefits

5. _____ Bicultural

6. _____ Bridge people

7. _____ Choices

8. _____ Cocoon

9. _____ Comfortably

10. _____ Culture of origin

11. _____ Diverse people

12. _____ Fractured

13. _____ Harmony

14. _____ Identity

15. _____ (to) Internalize

16. _____ Isolated

17. _____ (to) Mainstream

18. _____ Mutual understanding

19. _____ Peers

20. _____ Privilege

21. _____ (to) Recognize

22. _____ Relevant

23. _____ Rewards

24. _____ Social justice

25. _____ Stereotypes

26. _____ Tension

27. _____ (to) Thrive

Definitions

a. To grow in a healthy way

b. Living and working well together

c. A sheltered environment that is protected and safe

d. Options

e. The place where one is born

f. Something you deserve because you have worked hard for it

g. To do what is fair and right between peoples

h. Conflict

i. To know someone or something

j. Something that helps you

k. Combining two cultures

l. To change to fit into your surroundings

m. To look up to someone or something

n. People who are the same age

o. Broken

p. Someone who connects different people or groups

q. To like; to think positively or be thankful about someone or something

r. Easily; without problems

s. Who you are; the characteristics and qualities that define a person

t. A common picture in your head about a group of other people

u. Something that is related and that applies to the person or a situation

v. To take something within yourself

w. Understanding shared by two or more people

x. People of different cultures and backgrounds

y. The special opportunity to do or have something

z. To become part of the dominant culture

aa. To be alone, separated from

Choose seven of these vocabulary words and write a separate sentence for each word.

1. _____

2. _____

3. _____

4. _____

5. _____

6. _____

7. _____

Comprehension

1. What is a bicultural person?

2. Why are immigrants often hesitant to enter fully into their host culture?

3. What is a problem between the generations that can occur as a result?

4. What are the rewards of being a bicultural person?

Discussion

1. In what ways have you become a bicultural person?

2. If you have not, why do you think you are not?

3. What do you need to do to become bicultural?

4. In what ways have your children become bicultural?

5. What do you think are the advantages? The disadvantages?

6. Can you share a personal example of being a bridge builder between cultures?

Afterword—Some Notes for Teachers of the Curriculum

"Step by step the ladder is ascended."
—George Herbert

In this book, each chapter and topic has been like the rungs of a ladder, enabling students to increasingly understand the dominant culture that surrounds them and to have confidence to engage in that culture and thrive within it. The purpose of an English conversation approach (rather than a teacher-driven lecture or teaching approach) is so students can share their experiences and feelings with one another and discuss various coping strategies relevant to each topic. The hope is that they will grow together in confidence as they encourage each other to move in and out of mainstream culture. The teacher serves as a facilitator/director of that discussion-based approach and should not be the dominant presenter in the class.

The teacher of the curriculum can adapt the material to the specific mainstream culture of the students' context. It need not be limited to life in the United States. For example, chapter 15 on dominant American values can be changed to deal with the dominant values of the country in which the teacher and the students live. Similarly, the length of time that is spent on each chapter can be adapted according to the interests and needs of the students. A great deal of flexibility is built into the curriculum.

It is hoped that in every session, the teacher's own cross-cultural experiences will be added to the stories of the students. That allows the teacher to connect to the students and serve as a model in the bicultural identity process. He or she can also be a great encouragement to the students to keep working through the challenges of bicultural identity so they can enrich and be enriched by both cultures. That is literally living in the best of both worlds.

About the Author

In her career, Dr. Codman-Wilson has traveled and taught extensively in North America and Asia when she worked for ACMC (Association of Church Missions Committees) and WEF (World Evangelical Fellowship), respectively. In her last eleven years as senior pastor at Geneva Road/ Christ Community Church in Wheaton, Illinois, she had a co-pastor with her from the two-thirds world 70 percent of the time. One was a pastor from Nigeria, one a pastor from Malawi, and another a pastor/national worker from northeast India. There was also a youth worker from Indonesia and another from the Philippines. All except one were completing their graduate studies at Wheaton Graduate School before returning to their home countries. Her cross-cultural experience has also included immersion in the Asian-Indian community in Chicago. In addition, she and a Sri-Lankan college established the Chicago Ashram of Jesus Christ, where they held "Growing Up in America" seminars for first and second generation Indians and dialogue groups with Hindus, Buddhists, and Christians.

Her masters of theological studies is in Hindu-Buddhist-Christian dialogue. Her Ph.D. from Garrett Seminary/Northwestern University in Chicago is on Asian American identity issues and well-being. She has taught ESL using the curriculum that is in this book and material from her Ph.D. studies.

In August 2010, Dr. Codman-Wilson left the pastorate at Christ Community Church to pastor a multi-ethnic house church and continue discipleship, cross-cultural education, ESL teaching, and equipping Christians to be more effective communicators in word and deed in multicultural teams and contexts.

She and her husband live in the Chicago-land area as do their two grown children and their families.

ESL Glossary

Word/Definition   Chapter(s)

A

(to) Achieve (achievement): To earn a reward; success.   3, 15
(to) Adapt (adaptation): To change to fit into your surroundings   I, 1, 17
(to) Adjust: To change in order to fit   1, 14
Admire: To look up to someone or something   17
Allow: To say okay; to give permission   12
Alone: By itself or oneself   9
Alternative: Second choice (between two or more things)   4, 11
Anti-depressive medication: Medication for depression   13
Appreciate: To like, think positively, or be thankful about someone or something   17
Appropriately: In the right way for your setting   5
Assess: To measure; to evaluate   10
Assigned: Something given to do   5
(to) Assume: To take for granted; suppose something to be a fact   7
Assumption: Something we think or do without checking the facts   2
Attentively: Carefully, with one's full attention   5
Available: Can be gotten, had, or used   1
(to) Avoid: To keep away from; to keep from happening   4
Awkward: Feeling uncomfortable, embarrassed, or ashamed   4

B

Behavior: How a person acts   15
Benefits: Something that helps you   17
Bicultural: Combining two cultures   I, 17
(to) Blow out (candles): To put the fire out   16
Branches: The arms of a tree   16
Bravery: Courage   1
Bridge person: Someone who tries to connect different people or groups   7, 17
Bruise: A hurt on some part of the body   6
(to) Build trust: To work to understand another person so
    I am comfortable with him or her   3

C

Caucasian: A white person of Western European origin 7

Character: Moral qualities inside you 12

Choices: Options 17

Citizen: Belonging to a country, usually by birth 2

Citizenship: Acting with respect toward others 5

Clearly: Easily understood 5

Cocoon: A sheltered environment that is protected and safe I, 8, 17

Coherent: Makes sense 5

Comfortable: Freedom from care; feeling good I

Comfortably: Easily; without problems 17

Committed: Promise to do something, dedicated to a long-term course of action 7

(to) Communicate: To speak or make one's meaning known 2

(to) Complete: To finish 5, 11

(to) Comply: To accept or go along with 16

Comprehension: Understanding I, 5

(to) Conclude: To use what we know to make a decision 2

Confidence: Feeling sure of one's own abilities or the abilities of another I

Conform: To fit into 15

Constant: Not changing; remaining the same 14

Constructively: In a positive and helpful way 5

Context: The setting of words that helps you know what a word means I

(to) Continue: To keep on going 16

Convalescent center: A place where people get help after an illness or injury 2

Courage: Bravery 2

Creative: To make or do something new, showing imagination and inventiveness 11

Cultural traditions: Ways people act in your home country 16

Culture of origin: The place where one is born 17

Customs: Things people do as part of their culture 2, 13, 16

D

(to be) Defeated: To lose 8

(to) Defend: To stand for, speak on behalf of 11

Democracy: A society based on the equal rights of all people 15

(to) Demonstrate: To show 5

Dependable: Reliable all the time 12

Depression: Feelings of sadness, hopelessness, inadequacy 13

Destinations: Places you go to 15

(to) Describe: To tell about 16

Different: Not the same; unique 1, 2

Difficult: Hard 9, 14

Disappears: Goes away 13

Discouraged: Feeling like a failure; ready to give up 1, 8

E

F

G

H

(to) Handle: To take care of — I
(to) Happen: To take place — 2
Harmony: Living and working well together — 4, 17
(to) Hesitate: To pause or stop momentarily; to be unsure — 4
Honesty: Saying what one really thinks or feels, what is true — 4
(to) Honk: To make a loud noise — 9
Host: The person who invites you to his or her home or party — 4
(to be) Hired: To be employed for a job, get paid for a job — 12
Hurt: To feel injury or pain — 6

I

Identity: Who you are; the characteristics and qualities that define a person — I, 7, 17
(to) Illustrate: To picture the truth in a situation — 1
Impolite: Rude, not respectful — 4
Important: Something that means a lot, has value — 1, 12
Inadequate: Not able to complete a task successfully — 13
Incident: Something that happens — 2
Independently: Doing something or acting or thinking by oneself,
   not including others — 5
Indirect: To avoid a straightforward answer — 4
Inferior: Not good enough in comparison to others — 13
Inferential: Understanding the meaning that is being indirectly expressed — 5
(to) Interact: To work with someone or something — I
Interesting: Gets your attention or curiosity — 11
Intermediate: Between beginner and advanced; in the middle — I
International: A student or businessperson from one country
   visiting another country — 14
(to) Internalize: Take something within yourself — 17
(to) Involve: To include — I
Isolated: To be alone, separated from — 17
Isolation: Separation — 13
Issues: Topics people discuss or problems people face — I

J

Job performance: How well you do on a job — 12

L

M

N

O

P

R

S

Saris: Traditional Indian women's clothing 7
Satisfactory: Acceptable 10
Script: The written words to speak; the copy of a text 11
(to) Scold: To reprimand or discipline someone 15
Seasons: The patterns of the weather in a year 14
Self-control: Control over one's actions or feelings 5
Self-Evaluation: to review one's own effectiveness I
Self-sufficient: To be independent; to trust oneself 12
Sequences: What comes one after another 5
Shock: A sudden, bad surprise 14, 16
Shocked: Very surprised, often unpleasantly surprised 2
(to) Shout: To talk very loudly 16
Similar goals: Working to achieve the same things 3
Situations: The combination of circumstances at a given time; incidents that happen 11
Social justice: To do what is fair and right between peoples 17
Strategies: Skillful plans 5
Strengths: Areas of power; things one is good at 5
Stereotype: A common picture in your head about a group of other people I, 7, 17
(to) Struggle: To make one's way with great effort, to work hard 14
Subject matters: The areas of learning in school, like mathematics,
    social studies, and reading 5
Successfully: Doing something well I, 2
Suicide: To kill yourself 7
Suggestions: Ideas that are given for a situation 11
(to be) Surprised: To experience something unusual or unexpected 14
(to) Survive: To live at the most basic level 8

T

Tackle (in American football): to stop another person or throw them to the ground 8
"Talking about me behind my back": Gossip 2
Tardy: To be late 5
Team: A group of people who work together 7
Tension: Conflict 17
Think positively: To think about good things not bad things 13
(to) Thrive: To grow in a healthy way 8, 17
(to) Tip over: To fall down 16
(to) Tire: To be weary, to lose energy 9
Tragic: Something that brings suffering 7
Translator: Someone who explains the words in another language 6
Treatment: Help provided to get better from sickness 13

U

Unnecessary: Not needed 2

Unseen prompter: Someone or something (not seen) who directs
    your behavior or gives you cues about what to do or say   15
Usually: Most of the time; often   12

V

(to) Value: To see something as important; to treasure   2
Values: The social principles held or accepted by an individual, class, or society   15
Various: Different kinds of ways   I
Victim: Someone or something killed, hurt, or suffering
    by something that happens   7
Visitor: Someone who comes and then leaves or does not stay   1

W

(to) Walk a mile in their moccasins: To be able to understand
    what people are feeling   3
Welcomed: Invited into a person's life or home   3
Whenever: Anytime   7
Work habits: How a person does work, in a class environment or independently   5
Work permit: Paper giving permission for work   12
Worth the effort: The work you put into something is rewarded   8
Wounded: Hurt   9

X

X-rays: Pictures of the inside of the body   6

Sources Cited

Adeney, Bernard T. *Strange Virtues, Ethics in a Multicultural World*. IVP, 1995.

Augsburger, David W. *Pastoral Counseling Across Cultures*. Westminster Press, 1986.

Casse, Pierre and Deol, Surinder. *Managing Intercultural Negotiations*. Sietar International, 1985.

Codman-Wilson, M. L. (ed.) *Bridges, a Cross-Cultural Quarterly*. Summer. 1995.

—.*Thai Cultural and Religious Identity and Understanding of Well-Being in the United States: An Ethnographic Study of an Immigrant Church*. Unpublished Dissertation. Garrett/Northwestern University. 1992.

District 200 Board of Education, Wheaton, IL. *Parent's Guide to Report Cards,*4th Grade Report

Card. Community Unit School District 200.Web. 24 Aug 2011.

Hainsworth, F. Reed. "Precision and Dynamics of Positioning by Canada Geese Flying in

Formation."*Journal of Experimental Biology 128, 1986*.

Hecht, Joan. *The Journey of the Lost Boys*. Allswell Press, 2005.

United States. *Everyday Mysteries: Why do Geese Fly in a V?* 2010.

Bibliography

Adeney, Bernard T. *Strange Virtues, Ethics in a Multicultural World*. IVP, 1995.

Augsburger, David W. *Pastoral Counseling Across Cultures*. Westminster Press, 1986.

Casse, Pierre and Deol, Surinder. *Managing Intercultural Negotiations*. Sietar International, 1985.

Elmer, Duane. *Cross-Cultural Connections: Stepping out and Fitting in Around the World*. Intervarsity Press, 2002.

Gudykunst, William B. and Young Yun Kim. *Communicating with Strangers: An Approach to Intercultural Communication*.2nd Edition. McGraw Hill, 1992.

Hainsworth, F. Reed. "Precision and Dynamics of Positioning by Canada Geese Flying in Formation."*Journal of Experimental Biology 128, 1986*.

Hecht, Joan. *The Journey of the Lost Boys*. Allswell Press, 2005.

Hess, J. Daniel. *The Whole World Guide to Culture Learning*. Intercultural Press, 1994.

Kalb, Rosalind and Penelope Welch. *Moving Your Family Overseas*. Intercultural Press, 1992.

Kohls, L. Robert. *Survival Kit for Overseas Living*.3rd Edition. Intercultural Press, 1996.

Lane, Patty. *A Beginner's Guide to Crossing Cultures: Making Friends in a Multicultural World*. Intervarsity Press, 2002.

Laneir, Sarah A. *Foreign to Familiar*. McDougal Publishing, 2000.

Lingenfelter, Sherwood and Marvin Mayers. *Ministering Cross-Culturally*. Baker Book House, 1986.

Lonner, Walter J., and Roy S. Malpass. *Psychology and Culture*. Allyn and Bacon, 1994.

Nussbaum, Stan. *American Cultural Baggage: How to Recognize and Deal With It*. Orbis Books, 2005.

Phinney, Jean S. and Mary Jane Rotheram, Editors. *Children's Ethnic Socialization*. Sage Publications, 1987.

Pollock, David C. and Ruth E. Van Reken. *Third Culture Kids*. Nicholas Brealey Publishing/Intercultural Press, 2001.

Samovar, Larry A., Porter, Richard E., and Nemi C. Jain. *Understanding Intercultural Communication*. Wadsworth Publishing, 1981.

Stewart, Edward C and Milton J Bennett. *American Cultural Patterns: A Cross-cultural Perspective*. Intercultural Press, 1994.

Storti, Craig. *The Art of Crossing Cultures*. 2nd edition. Intercultural Press, 2001.

—. *Figuring Foreigners Out: A Practical Guide*. Intercultural Press, 1999.